MARK TWAIN AND THE MISSISSIPPI RIVER:

How the River Impacted Twain's Life, Career, and Writings.

by Bill Wiemuth

HISTORYHIGHLIGHTS.COM PRESENTS

MARK TWAIN
AND THE
MISSISSIPPI RIVER:

How the River Impacted
Twain's Life, Career, and Writings.

Published by
HistoryHighlights.com
Fascinating true stories in less than an hour.
For the curious mind without a lot of time.
— Online Multimedia Presentations —
— eBooks — Paperbacks — Audiobooks —

Visit **HistoryHighlights.com**
and sample our recent newsletters,
plus receive free books, video presentations,
and updates about new releases.

ACCOLADES

An incredibly important and fascinating saga in our nation's history, told by the master of US history storytelling.
– Trudy Cusack

My husband told me if he had attended a history class in high school given by someone like you, he probably would have gone on to school and become a history teacher.
– Joy Snider

Bill Wiemuth is able to do what so many historians cannot. He can take history and put it in a form that is not only enjoyable but makes you want more.
– David

Bill, your knowledge of the history of our country is second to none and your presentation of the material was entertaining as well as informative.
– Sally and Fred Burner

Bill's ability to entwine the river and history, and a bit of fun, really brought to life each event. The historical background on these issues was both interesting and educational.
– Lon and Kathy Willmann

CONTENTS

INTRODUCTION 5

YOUTH ALONG THE RIVER 7

A CAREER-CHANGING STEAMBOAT TRIP 13

LEARNING TO BE A RIVER PILOT 16

THE MISSISSIPPI RIVER 21

THE STEAMBOAT ERA 29

A TYRANT PILOT 36

BROTHER HENRY 40

A "FULL-FLEDGED" PILOT 43

BECOMING MARK TWAIN 46

RIVER WRITINGS 49

LATER LIFE 52

CLOSING 56

Please – A Quick Review. 59

Learn More 60

About the Author 62

INTRODUCTION

Mark Twain, courtesy of Wikimedia Commons

More than a century after his death, Mark Twain remains one of the most iconic Americans in history. His talent as a writer produced a trove of treasured literary-masterpieces. Audiences packed auditoriums for Twain's humorous and insightful lectures. He traveled around the globe at a time when that was relatively uncommon and always captured his subject with eloquence and unique perspective.

In this book, you will discover how America's waterways – especially the Mississippi River – significantly impacted Mark Twain's life, career, and writings.

Welcome to this History Highlights book. My name is Bill Wiemuth and I am excited to share with you this amazing story about one of the great American icons.

If you have a curious mind, but not a lot of time, you have made the perfect decision to join me. If you love fascinating true stories of intriguing people and incredible events that shaped the history of the United States, then you are in the right place.

At HistoryHighlights.com, enjoy our FREE weekly newsletter with free eBooks, video presentations, and updates about our ongoing development of new eBooks, audiobooks, and multimedia programs! Learn more at **HistoryHighlights.com**.

A love of history grows into a thrilling passion. So, get ready to fall in love with history – again or for the first time. Experience wonder. Revel in these incredible tales of remarkable people and events that shaped – and continue to shape – the United States. Visit **HistoryHighlights.com** to explore great stories from history.

Get ready for a journey of discovery.

YOUTH ALONG THE RIVER

Sam Clemens at age 14 in 1850 holding a printer's composing stick with letters SAM. Courtesy of Wikimedia Commons.

Many people are aware that Mark Twain's youth was spent along the banks of the Mississippi River at Hannibal, Missouri. But he was not born as Mark Twain nor born at Hannibal. He was actually born in Florida... Florida, Missouri, about 30 miles west of Hannibal.

He was born November 30, 1835, as Samuel Langhorn Clemens to parents Jane and John Clemens. That autumn, a strange omen hovered in the skies as Halley's Comet made its journey across the heavens.

Sam's father was an attorney and justice of peace. When Sam was only three years old, the family in 1839 moved to Hannibal, where Sam spent the next 14 years of his life along the banks of the Mississippi River. But when Sam was only 11, his father died. To help support the family, Sam left school at age 13 to apprentice to the local printer.

Much of Sam's labor was dedicated to the tedious process of setting type in preparation for the printing press. For every handwritten passage, Sam would remove each individual letter and mark of punctuation from drawers of type and tediously assemble them backwards - from right to left - so after being inked and stamped onto paper the image was readable. The work was dull and mind-numbing. It is understandable that young Sam dreamed of other pursuits. Many of his daydreams focused around the colorful and exciting life of working aboard paddlewheel steamboats on the Mississippi River. In his book *Life on the Mississippi,* he wrote:

> *When I was a boy, there was but one permanent ambition among my comrades in our village on the west bank of the Mississippi River. That was, to be a steamboatman. We had transient ambitions of other sorts, but they were only transient. When a circus came and went, it left us all burning to become*

*clowns; the first minstrel show that came to our
section left us all suffering to try that kind of life;
now and then we had a hope that if we lived and
were good, God would permit us to be pirates. These
ambitions faded out, each in its turn; but the
ambition to be a steamboatman always remained.*

The river maintained a constant influence on life in
Hannibal, Missouri. Twain described how the flurry of
activity caused by the arrival of a steamboat could
transform the town:

*After all these years I can picture that old time to
myself now, just as it was then: the white town
drowsing in the sunshine of a summer's morning;
the streets empty, or pretty nearly so...the majestic,
the magnificent Mississippi, rolling its mile-wide
tide along, shining in the sun...*

*Presently a film of dark smoke appears... instantly a
drayman, famous for his quick eye and prodigious
voice, lifts up the cry, "S-t-e-a-m-boat a-comin'!"
and the scene changes!*

*The town drunkard stirs, the clerks wake up, a
furious clatter of drays follows, every house and store
pours out a human contribution, and all in a
twinkling the dead town is alive and moving.*

*Drays, carts, men, boys, all go hurrying from many
quarters to a common center, the wharf. Assembled
there, the people fasten their eyes upon the coming
boat as upon a wonder they are seeing for the first*

time. And the boat IS rather a handsome sight, too. She is long and sharp and trim and pretty; she has two tall, fancy-topped chimneys...; a fanciful pilot-house... perched on top... the upper decks are filled with passengers;

...the captain stands by the big bell, calm, imposing, the envy of all; ...the broad stage is run far out over the port bow, and an envied deckhand stands picturesquely on the end of it with a coil of rope in his hand; the captain lifts his hand, a bell rings, the wheels stop; then they turn back, churning the water to foam, and the steamer is at rest.

Then such a scramble as there is to get aboard, and to get ashore, and to take in freight and to discharge freight, all at one and the same time; and such a yelling and cursing as the mates facilitate it all with! Ten minutes later the steamer is under way again... After ten more minutes the town is dead again, and the town drunkard asleep by the skids once more.

The action at the riverfront was not the only appeal. The colorful characters that worked at the riverfront and on board the steamboats were drastically different from the reserved residents of Hannibal. Twain described them as:

...hordes of rough and hardy men; rude, uneducated, brave, suffering terrific hardships with sailor-like stoicism; heavy drinkers, coarse frolickers in moral sties like the Natchez-under-the-hill of that day,

heavy fighters, reckless fellows, every one, elephantinely jolly, foul-witted, profane; prodigal of their money, bankrupt at the end of the trip, fond of barbaric finery, prodigious braggarts; yet, in the main, honest, trustworthy, faithful to promises and duty, and often picturesquely magnanimous.

The excitement and the characters of the riverboats were too much to resist for young Sam Clemens. Late in his life, he recounted the story of his first ride on a steamboat when he was only seven. The interview was published in the *New York World* edition of September 7, 1902:

Do you know what it means to be a boy on the banks of the Mississippi, to see the steamboats go up and down the river, and never to have had a ride on one? ...Well, I was seven years old and my dream by night and my longing by day had never been realized...

One day when the big packet that used to stop at Hannibal rung up to the mooring at my native town, a small chunk of a lad might have been seen kiting on to the deck and in a jiffy disappearing from view beneath a yawl that was placed bottom up. I was the small chunk of a lad.

...Well, the packet started along all right, and it gave me great thrills of joy to be on a real sure-enough steamboat.

...seventeen miles below Hannibal, I was discovered by one of the crew. They put me ashore...[and] I was

sent home by some friends of my father's. My father
met me on my return.

At age 17, Sam Clemens left Hannibal, Missouri in pursuit of a life of adventure. He still nurtured his lifelong dream to work on the riverboats. He wrote, "So by and by I ran away. I said I never would come home again till I was a pilot and could come in glory. But somehow I could not manage it."

A CAREER-CHANGING STEAMBOAT TRIP

Mark Twain in 1851, courtesy of Wikimedia Commons.

After leaving Hannibal at age 17, Sam Clemens began to drift from town to town and job to job. Working jobs in the printing trade, he resided for a while in St. Louis, Philadelphia, and New York City. He worked briefly for his older brother Orion at newspapers in Hannibal, Missouri, and at Muscatine and Keokuk, Iowa.

By April of 1857 Sam was living in Cincinnati, Ohio and had decided to embark upon a new adventure. Always a voracious reader, Sam had read that the upper regions of South America's Amazon River had not yet been fully explored. Sam envisioned himself as the explorer to accomplish that task. So, he packed his belongings and bought a ticket on a steamboat bound for New Orleans. There he planned to purchase passage on a ship to South America. He wrote:

I packed my valise, and took passage on an ancient tub called the 'Paul Jones,' for New Orleans...When we presently got under way and went poking down the broad Ohio [River], I became a new being, and the subject of my own admiration. I was a traveler! A word never had tasted so good in my mouth before. I had an exultant sense of being bound for mysterious lands and distant climes which I never have felt in so uplifting a degree since.

Thankfully, Clemens did not travel all the way to South America. The 1300-mile journey aboard the steamboat *Paul Jones* from Cincinnati down the Ohio and Mississippi Rivers to New Orleans altered his plans. Clemens' childhood dreams were reawakened and he rededicated his efforts to securing an opportunity to learn to be a riverboat pilot: He wrote:

What with ...some delays, the poor old "Paul Jones" fooled away about two weeks in making the voyage from Cincinnati to New Orleans.

This gave me a chance to get acquainted with one of the pilots, and he taught me how to steer the boat, and thus made the fascination of river life more potent than ever for me... Therefore it followed that I must contrive a new career.

The "Paul Jones" was now bound for St. Louis. I planned a siege against my pilot, and at the end of three hard days he surrendered. He agreed to teach me the Mississippi River from New Orleans to St. Louis for five hundred dollars, payable out of the first wages I should receive after graduating.

LEARNING TO BE A RIVER PILOT

Steamboat pilot Horace Bixby agreed to teach Sam to navigate the river and pilot a riverboat. Aboard the steamboat *Pennsylvania*, young Sam began his training.

I entered upon the small enterprise of "learning" twelve or thirteen hundred miles of the great Mississippi River with the easy confidence of my time of life. If I had really known what I was about to require of my faculties, I should not have had the courage to begin. I supposed that all a pilot had to do was to keep his boat in the river, and I did not consider that that could be much of a trick, since it was so wide...

Sam recorded that Bixby quickly gave him specific instructions:

"My boy, you must get a little memorandum-book, and every time I tell you a thing, put it down right away. There's only one way to be a pilot, and that is to get this entire river by heart. You have to know it just like A B C."

As Sam realized he was expected to memorize every curve, bend, log jam, sunken steamboat wreck, and shifting sandbar for 1,200 miles of river between New

Orleans and St. Louis, he dejectedly wrote, "That was a dismal revelation to me; for my memory was never loaded with anything but blank cartridges."

Sam went on to describe the remarkable skills requisite in a steamboat pilot. He wrote:

> *Two things seemed pretty apparent to me. One was, that in order to be a pilot a man had got to learn more than any one man ought to be allowed to know; and the other was, that he must learn it all over again in a different way every twenty-four hours.*

Due to frequent - and often drastic - fluctuation in water levels influenced by every varying season of snowmelt and rainfall, every journey along the Mississippi River presents new navigational challenges. Sam described the challenges this way:

> *...There is one faculty which a pilot must incessantly cultivate until he has brought it to absolute perfection. Nothing short of perfection will do. That faculty is memory. He cannot stop with merely thinking a thing is so and so; he must know it; for this is eminently one of the 'exact' sciences...*

> *I think a pilot's memory is about the most wonderful thing in the world. To know the Old and New Testaments by heart, and be able to recite them glibly, forward or backward, or begin at random anywhere in the book and recite both ways and never trip or make a mistake, is no extravagant mass of knowledge, and no marvelous facility, compared to a*

pilot's massed knowledge of the Mississippi and his marvelous facility in the handling of it. I make this comparison deliberately, and believe I am not expanding the truth when I do it. Many will think my figure too strong, but pilots will not.

...A pilot must have a memory; but there are two higher qualities which he must also have. He must have good and quick judgment and decision, and a cool, calm courage that no peril can shake. Give a man the merest trifle of pluck to start with, and by the time he has become a pilot he cannot be unmanned by any danger a steamboat can get into; but one cannot quite say the same for judgment. Judgment is a matter of brains, and a man must START with a good stock of that article or he will never succeed as a pilot.

As Sam proceeded in his training, study, and confidence. Mr. Bixby prepared for him a challenge:

...At the end of what seemed a tedious while, I had managed to pack my head full of islands, towns, bars, 'points,' and bends... But of course my complacency could hardly get start enough to lift my nose a trifle into the air before Mr. Bixby would think of something to fetch it down again.

One day he turned on me suddenly with this settler--

"What is the shape of Walnut Bend?"

He might as well have asked me my grandmother's opinion of protoplasm. I reflected respectfully, and then said I didn't know it had any particular shape.

...By and by he said--

"My boy, you've got to know the SHAPE of the river perfectly. It is all there is left to steer by on a very dark night. Everything else is blotted out and gone. But mind you, it hasn't the same shape in the night that it has in the day-time.

"...You see, this has got to be learned; there isn't any getting around it. A clear starlight night throws such heavy shadows that if you didn't know the shape of a shore perfectly you would claw away from every bunch of timber, because you would take the black shadow of it for a solid cape; and you see you would be getting scared to death every fifteen minutes by the watch. You would be fifty yards from shore all the time when you ought to be within fifty feet of it. You can't see a snag in one of those shadows, but you know exactly where it is, and the shape of the river tells you when you are coming to it.

"Then there's your pitch-dark night; the river is a very different shape on a pitch-dark night from what it is on a starlight night. All shores seem to be straight lines, then, and mighty dim ones, too; and you'd RUN them for straight lines only you know better. You boldly drive your boat right into what seems to be a solid, straight wall (you knowing very

well that in reality there is a curve there), and that wall falls back and makes way for you.

"Then there's your gray mist. You take a night when there's one of these grisly, drizzly, gray mists, and then there isn't any particular shape to a shore. A gray mist would tangle the head of the oldest man that ever lived. Well, then, different kinds of MOONLIGHT change the shape of the river in different ways. You see -- --"

I interrupted him and begged, "Oh, don't say any more, please! Have I got to learn the shape of the river according to all these five hundred thousand different ways? If I tried to carry all that cargo in my head it would make me stoop-shouldered."

"NO!" he said "You only learn THE shape of the river, and you learn it with such absolute certainty that you can always steer by the shape that's IN YOUR HEAD, and never mind the one that's before your eyes."

I told him... "I want to retire from this business. I want a slush-bucket and a brush; I'm only fit for a roustabout. I haven't got brains enough to be a pilot; and if I had I wouldn't have strength enough to carry them around unless I went on crutches."

He replied to me firmly, "Now drop that! When I say I'll learn a man the river, I mean it. And you can depend on it, I'll learn him or kill him."

THE MISSISSIPPI RIVER

Twain's study of the river grew into a passion. The river's history and environment is endlessly fascinating. He wrote, "The Mississippi is well worth reading about. It is not a commonplace river, but on the contrary is in all ways remarkable."

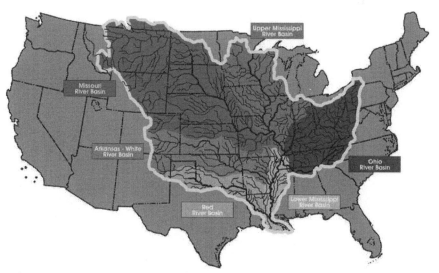

The Mississippi River drainage basin, courtesy of Wikimedia Commons.

The Mississippi River collects hundreds of tributary rivers draining 1.2 million square miles of land between the Rocky Mountains and the Appalachian Mountains. This creates an extensive network of rivers serving as avenues of transportation throughout the interior of the continent. Twain reported, "The Mississippi receives and carries to the Gulf water from fifty-four subordinate rivers that are navigable by steamboats, and from some hundreds that are navigable by flats and keels."

Along its 2,350-mile journey, the Mississippi River descends only 1,450 feet in elevation. During its last 700 miles from Memphis to the Gulf of Mexico, the river drops an average of only three inches per mile. Traveling so gradually downhill through a muddy floodplain the river meanders in long sweeping curves. Twain describes it in a way only he could:

> *It seems safe to say that it is also the crookedest river in the world, since in one part of its journey it uses up one thousand three hundred miles to cover the same ground that the crow would fly over in six hundred and seventy-five...*

> *The Mississippi is remarkable in still another way -- its disposition to make prodigious jumps by cutting through narrow necks of land, and thus straightening and shortening itself...*

> *In the space of one hundred and seventy-six years the Lower Mississippi has shortened itself two hundred and forty-two miles. That is an average of a trifle over one mile and a third per year. Therefore, any calm person... can see that...just a million years ago next November, the Lower Mississippi River was upwards of one million three hundred thousand miles long, and stuck out over the Gulf of Mexico*

like a fishing-rod. And by the same token any person can see that seven hundred and forty-two years from now the Lower Mississippi will be only a mile and three-quarters long... There is something fascinating about science. One gets such wholesale returns of conjecture out of such a trifling investment of fact.

In addition to the river's natural characteristics, Twain also was intrigued by its role as an avenue of exploration and development. He wrote:

Let us drop the Mississippi's physical history, and say a word about its historical history -- so to speak.

...We do of course know that there are several comparatively old dates in American history, but the mere figures convey to our minds no just idea, no distinct realization, of the stretch of time which they represent. To say that De Soto, the first white man who ever saw the Mississippi River, saw it in 1542, is a remark which states a fact without interpreting it: it is something like giving the dimensions of a sunset by astronomical measurements, and cataloging the colors by their scientific names; -- as a result, you get the bald fact of the sunset, but you don't see the sunset. It would have been better to paint a picture of it.

Unquestionably the discovery of the Mississippi is a date-able fact which considerably mellows and modifies the shiny newness of our country, and gives

her a most respectable outside-aspect of rustiness and
antiquity.

De Soto merely glimpsed the river, then died and
was buried in it by his priests and soldiers... The
Mississippi was left unvisited by whites during a
term of years which seems incredible in our energetic
days. One may 'sense' the interval to his mind, after
a fashion, by dividing it up in this way: After De
Soto glimpsed the river, a fraction short of a quarter
of a century elapsed, and then Shakespeare was born;
lived a trifle more than half a century, then died; and
when he had been in his grave considerably more
than half a century, the SECOND white man saw
the Mississippi. In our day we don't allow a hundred
and thirty years to elapse between glimpses of a
marvel...

...Apparently nobody happened to want such a river,
nobody needed it, nobody was curious about it; so,
for a century and a half the Mississippi remained out
of the market and undisturbed...

But at last La Salle the Frenchman conceived the idea
of seeking out that river and exploring it.

...Naturally the question suggests itself, Why did
these people want the river now when nobody had
wanted it in the five preceding generations?
Apparently it was because at this late day they
thought they had discovered a way to make it useful;
for it had come to be believed that the Mississippi

emptied into the Gulf of California, and therefore afforded a short cut from Canada to China...

...In 1673 Joliet the merchant, and Marquette the priest, crossed the country and reached the banks of the Mississippi.

They... proved to their satisfaction, that the Mississippi did not empty into the Gulf of California, or into the Atlantic. They believed it emptied into the Gulf of Mexico. They turned back, now, and carried their great news to Canada.

But belief is not proof. It was reserved for La Salle to furnish the proof. He...at last got his expedition under way at the end of the year 1681.

Day by day they floated down the great bends, in the shadow of the dense forests...The voyagers journeyed on, touching here and there; 'passed the sites, since become historic, of Vicksburg and Grand Gulf,' ...

The voyagers visited the Natchez Indians, near the site of the present city of that name...

A few more days swept swiftly by, and La Salle stood in the shadow of his confiscating cross... with the waters of the Gulf of Mexico, his task finished...

...Seventy years elapsed, after the exploration, before the river's borders had a white population worth considering; and nearly fifty more before the river had a commerce. Between La Salle's opening of the river and the time when it may be said to have become the vehicle of anything like a regular and

active commerce, seven sovereigns had occupied the throne of England, America had become an independent nation, Louis XIV and Louis XV had...died, the French monarchy had gone down in the red tempest of the revolution, and Napoleon was a name that was beginning to be talked about. Truly, there were snails in those days.

The lore and mystery and scenery of the Mississippi River is mesmerizing. Twain wrote so beautifully about the river. Here is a lovely passage about the gorgeous upper portion of the Mississippi River:

We move up the river -- always through enchanting scenery, there being no other kind on the Upper Mississippi...

The majestic bluffs that overlook the river, along through this region, charm one with the grace and variety of their forms, and the soft beauty of their adornment. The steep verdant slope, whose base is at the water's edge is topped by a lofty rampart of broken, turreted rocks, which are exquisitely rich and mellow in color -- mainly dark browns and dull greens, but splashed with other tints.

Twain wrote of the magic that the river provides:

...you have the shining river, winding here and there and yonder, its sweep interrupted at intervals by clusters of wooded islands threaded by silver channels; and you have glimpses of distant villages,

asleep upon capes...in the shade of the forest walls;
and of white steamers vanishing around remote
points. And it is all as tranquil and reposeful as
dreamland, and has nothing this-worldly about it --
nothing to hang a fret or a worry upon.

Sometimes on the river, something as simple and lovely as a sunset can be elevated to a transcendent experience. Twain captured it beautifully in this passage:

I still keep in mind a certain wonderful sunset which
I witnessed when steamboating was new to me. A
broad expanse of the river was turned to blood; in the
middle distance the red hue brightened into gold,
through which a solitary log came floating, black and
conspicuous; in one place a long, slanting mark lay
sparkling upon the water; in another the surface was
broken by boiling, tumbling rings, that were as
many-tinted as an opal; where the ruddy flush was
faintest, was a smooth spot that was covered with
graceful circles and radiating lines, ever so delicately
traced; the shore on our left was densely wooded, and
the somber shadow that fell from this forest was
broken in one place by a long, ruffled trail that shone
like silver; and high above the forest wall a clean-
stemmed dead tree waved a single leafy bough that
glowed like a flame in the unobstructed splendor that
was flowing from the sun. There were graceful
curves, reflected images, woody heights, soft
distances; and over the whole scene, far and near, the

dissolving lights drifted steadily, enriching it, every passing moment, with new marvels of coloring.

I stood like one bewitched. I drank it in, in a speechless rapture. The world was new to me, and I had never seen anything like this at home.

THE STEAMBOAT ERA

Early river vessels, courtesy of Wikimedia Commons.

The river's earliest commerce was in great barges --
flatboats and keelboats. These were floated from the
upper river and myriad tributaries to New Orleans.
Along with their cargos, the boats frequently were sold
for scrap lumber. Rowing, poling, or dragging boats back
upstream was extremely slow and laborious. A voyage
downstream and the return journey back could require
up to nine months. Over time this commerce increased,
providing employment to hordes of rough and hardy
men. As keelboats faded away, the boatsmen transitioned
to serve as deck hands, or a mate, or a pilot on the
steamers.

As Sam Clemens left the small steamer called the *Paul Jones* to move with Horace Bixby to a larger steamboat, he was amazed at the grandeur of the vessel:

She was a grand affair. When I stood in her pilot-house I was so far above the water that I seemed perched on a mountain; and her decks stretched so far away, fore and aft, below me, that I wondered how I could ever have considered the little 'Paul Jones' a large craft. There were other differences, too. The 'Paul Jones's' pilot-house was a cheap, dingy, battered rattle-trap, cramped for room: but here was a sumptuous glass temple; room enough to have a dance in; showy red and gold window-curtains; an imposing sofa; leather cushions and a back to the high bench where visiting pilots sit, to spin yarns and 'look at the river;...

I began to take heart once more to believe that piloting was a romantic sort of occupation after all. The moment we were under way I began to prowl about the great steamer and fill myself with joy. She was as clean and as dainty as a drawing-room; when I looked down her long, gilded saloon, it was like gazing through a splendid tunnel; she had an oil-picture, by some gifted sign-painter, on every stateroom door; she glittered with no end of prism-fringed chandeliers; the clerk's office was elegant, the bar was marvelous, and the bar-keeper had been barbered and upholstered at incredible cost. The boiler deck (i.e. the second story of the boat, so to

*speak) was as spacious as a church, it seemed to me;
...I had never felt so fine before.*

*When he stepped aboard a big fine steamboat, he
entered a new and marvelous world: ...all garnished
with white wooden filigree work of fanciful
patterns;...gilt deer-horns over the big bell;...big
roomy boiler-deck, painted blue, and furnished with
Windsor armchairs; inside, a far-receding snow-
white 'cabin;' ... curving patterns of filigree-work
touched up with gilding, stretching overhead all
down the converging vista; big chandeliers every
little way, each an April shower of glittering glass-
drops; lovely rainbow-light falling everywhere from
the colored glazing of the skylights; the whole a long-
drawn, resplendent tunnel, a bewildering and soul-
satisfying spectacle!*

*A busy landing with several steamboats. Courtesy of
Wikimedia Commons.*

Steamboats occasionally raced each other for publicity and acclaim. Twain loved the experience and described the events as only he could:

I think that much the most enjoyable of all races is a steamboat race... Two red--hot steamboats raging along, neck-and-neck, straining every nerve--that is to say, every rivet in the boilers--quaking and shaking and groaning from stem to stern, spouting white steam from the pipes, pouring black smoke from the chimneys, raining down sparks, parting the river into long breaks of hissing foam--this is sport that makes a body's very liver curl with enjoyment...

The steamboats "Natchez" and "Robert E. Lee" depicted during their famous 1870 race. Courtesy of Wikimedia Commons.

In the following passage, Twain provides more details about why boats raced, the endeavors of those competitions, and the excitement manifested along the river:

In the 'flush times' of steamboating, a race between two notoriously fleet steamers was an event of vast importance. The date was set for it several weeks in advance, and from that time forward, the whole Mississippi Valley was in a state of consuming excitement. Politics and the weather were dropped, and people talked only of the coming race. As the time approached, the two steamers 'stripped' and got ready. Every encumbrance that added weight, or exposed a resisting surface to wind or water, was removed, if the boat could possibly do without it.

...When the 'Eclipse' and the 'A. L. Shotwell' ran their great race many years ago, it was said that pains were taken to scrape the gilding off the fanciful device which hung between the 'Eclipse's' chimneys, and that for that one trip the captain ...had his head shaved. But I always doubted these things.

...Hardly any passengers were taken, ...No way-freights and no way-passengers were allowed, for the racers would stop only at the largest towns, and then it would be only 'touch and go.' Coal flats and wood flats were contracted for beforehand, and these were kept ready to hitch on to the flying steamers at a moment's warning. Double crews were carried, so that all work could be quickly done.

The chosen date being come, and all things in readiness, the two great steamers back into the stream, and lie there jockeying a moment, and apparently watching each other's slightest movement, like sentient creatures; flags drooping, the pent steam shrieking through safety-valves, the black smoke rolling and tumbling from the chimneys and darkening all the air. People, people everywhere; the shores, the house-tops, the steamboats, the ships, are packed with them, and you know that the borders of the broad Mississippi are going to be fringed with humanity thence northward twelve hundred miles, to welcome these racers.

Presently tall columns of steam burst from the 'scape-pipes of both steamers, two guns boom a good-bye, two red-shirted heroes mounted on capstans wave their small flags above the massed crews on the forecastles, two plaintive solos linger on the air a few waiting seconds, two mighty choruses burst forth -- and here they come! Brass bands bray Hail Columbia, huzza after huzza thunders from the shores, and the stately creatures go whistling by like the wind.

...Two nicely matched steamers will stay in sight of each other day after day. They might even stay side by side, but for the fact that pilots are not all alike, and the smartest pilots will win the race. If one of the boats has a 'lightning' pilot, whose 'partner' is a trifle his inferior, you can tell which one is on watch by noting whether that boat has gained ground or

lost some during each four-hour stretch. The shrewdest pilot can delay a boat if he has not a fine genius for steering. Steering is a very high art...

There is a great difference in boats, of course. For a long time I was on a boat that was so slow we used to forget what year it was we left port in... Ferryboats used to lose valuable trips because their passengers grew old and died, waiting for us to get by...

A TYRANT PILOT

During Sam's training to learn the river, his mentor
Horace Bixby accepted a job offer to pilot along the
notoriously dangerous Missouri River. But Bixby ordered
Sam to remain on the Mississippi River to continue
studying the 1,200 miles between New Orleans and St.
Louis. Sam was assigned to study under the instruction
of pilot William Brown. The personalities of the student
and teacher were not well-suited. This is how Sam
described Brown:

*He was a middle-aged, long, slim, bony, smooth-
shaven, horse-faced, ignorant, stingy, malicious,
snarling, fault hunting, mote-magnifying tyrant. I
early got the habit of coming on watch with dread at
my heart.*

*Brown was ALWAYS watching for a pretext to find
fault; and if he could find no plausible pretext, he
would invent one. He would scold you for shaving a
shore, and for not shaving it; for hugging a bar, and
for not hugging it; for 'pulling down' when not
invited, and for not pulling down when not invited;
for firing up without orders, and for waiting FOR
orders. In a word, it was his invariable rule to find
fault with EVERYTHING you did; and another*

invariable rule of his was to throw all his remarks (to you) into the form of an insult.

The tensions increased between Sam and Brown until Sam wrote:

I often wanted to kill Brown, but this would not answer. A cub had to take everything his boss gave, in the way of vigorous comment and criticism;

However, I could IMAGINE myself killing Brown; there was no law against that; and that was the thing I used always to do the moment I was abed. Instead of going over my river in my mind as was my duty, I threw business aside for pleasure, and killed Brown. I killed Brown every night for months; not in old, stale, commonplace ways, but in new and picturesque ones; -- ways that were sometimes surprising for freshness of design and ghastliness of situation and environment.

Sam helped his younger brother Henry Clemens acquire a job onboard the steamboat *Pennsylvania.* Henry eventually got caught in the storm of Brown's wrath. Sam recounted the story:

...I got into serious trouble. Brown was steering; I was 'pulling down.' My younger brother appeared on the hurricane deck, and shouted to Brown to stop at some landing or other a mile or so below. Brown gave no intimation that he had heard anything. But that was his way: he never condescended to take

*notice of an under clerk. The wind was blowing;
Brown was deaf (although he always pretended he
wasn't), and I very much doubted if he had heard the
order. If I had two heads, I would have spoken; but as
I had only one, it seemed judicious to take care of it;
so I kept still.*

*Presently, sure enough, we went sailing by that
plantation. Captain Klinefelter appeared on the
deck...and he inquired as to why we had not stopped.
Brown said Henry came up but never told him told
to stop. The Captain asked me and even though I did
not want to get involved, I answered that he had.*

*An hour later, Henry entered the pilot-house,
unaware of what had been going on. He was a
thoroughly inoffensive boy, and I was sorry to see
him come, for I knew Brown would have no pity on
him. Brown began, straightway ...he called Henry a
liar and ordered him out of the Pilot House.*

*The boy started out, and even had his foot on the
upper step outside the door, when Brown, with a
sudden access of fury, picked up a ten-pound lump of
coal and sprang after him; but I was between, with a
heavy stool, and I hit Brown a good honest blow
which stretched-him out.*

*I had committed the crime of crimes -- I had lifted my
hand against a pilot on duty! I supposed I was
booked for the penitentiary sure, and couldn't be
booked any surer if I went on and squared my long
account with this person while I had the chance;*

consequently I stuck to him and pounded him with my fists a considerable time -- I do not know how long, the pleasure of it probably made it seem longer than it really was; -- but in the end he struggled free and jumped up and sprang to the wheel: a very natural solicitude, for, all this time, here was this steamboat tearing down the river at the rate of fifteen miles an hour and nobody at the helm! ...the boat was steering herself straight down the middle and taking no chances. Still, that was only luck -- a body MIGHT have found her charging into the woods.

The racket had brought everybody to the hurricane deck, and I trembled when I saw the old captain looking up from the midst of the crowd.

...I followed the Captain to his quarters. After asking me what had happened, to which I answered honestly, the Captain remarked,

"I'm deuced glad of it! Hark ye, never mention that I said that. You have been guilty of a great crime; and don't you ever be guilty of it again, on this boat. BUT -- lay for him ashore! Give him a good sound thrashing, do you hear? I'll pay the expenses. Now go -- and mind you, not a word of this to anybody..."

When Brown came off watch he went straight to the captain...and demanded that I be put ashore in New Orleans...

BROTHER HENRY

Henry Clemens. Courtesy of WikiTree.com

After Sam's fight with pilot William Brown and Brown's insistence that Sam be fired, the Captain remarked that he'd prefer to fire Brown. But another available pilot could not be located. So, the captain arranged for Sam to travel from New Orleans to St. Louis on the steamboat *A. T. Lacey*. The captain told Sam that he planned to telegraph ahead to St. Louis and locate a pilot to replace Brown. When Sam arrived aboard the *A. T. Lacey,* he could then return to his steersman training position aboard the *Pennsylvania* with the new pilot.

That night in New Orleans, the two brothers, Sam and Henry, sat on the New Orleans levee smoking cigars and reviewing the drama.

Henry departed aboard the steamboat *Pennsylvania,* along with Captain Klinefelter and William Brown. Sam moved to the *A.T. Lacey,* which departed New Orleans a couple of days after the *Pennsylvania.*

When Sam arrived at Greenville, Mississippi, he learned news that about 60 miles below Memphis, the *Pennsylvania* had exploded on June 13, 1858. Sam had no idea what had happened to his brother until he arrived in Memphis two days after the explosion and located his severely-injured and unconscious brother. Sam learned from other surviving crew members that the explosion had blasted Henry off the boat and he and others had floated on wreckage to shore. But since Henry had grown up on the banks of the Mississippi River, he had learned to swim. He swam back to the burning wreck of the *Pennsylvania* to try and assist others and was subsequently terribly burned.

On June 18, 1858, Sam wrote a letter to inform his family of the accident. He penned the letter to his sister-in-law Mollie Clemens, the wife of his older brother Orion. He wrote:

> *...lost and ruined sinner as I am--I, even I, have humbled myself to the ground and prayed as never man prayed before, that the great God might let this*

cup pass from me,--that he would strike me to the earth, but spare my brother--that he would pour out the fullness of his just wrath upon my wicked head, but have mercy, mercy, mercy upon that unoffending boy. The horrors of three days have swept over me-- they have blasted my youth and left me an old man before my time. Mollie, there are grey hairs in my head to-night. For forty-eight hours I labored at the bedside of my poor burned and bruised, but uncomplaining brother, and then the star of my hope went out and left me in the gloom of despair. Then poor wretched me, that was once so proud, was humbled to the very dust,--lower than the dust--for the vilest beggar in the streets of Saint Louis could never conceive of a humiliation like mine. Men take me by the hand and congratulate me, and call me "lucky" because I was not on the "Pennsylvania" when she blew up! My God forgive them, for they know not what they say.

At age 19, young Henry Clemens died on June 21, 1858. He was one of more than 100 that perished in the accident.

A "FULL-FLEDGED" PILOT

Statue of Sam Clemens (Mark Twain) at a riverboat steering wheel. Courtesy of Wikimedia Commons.

Grieving the loss of his brother, Sam Clemens continued his piloting study along the Mississippi River. After 17 months of apprenticeship, he passed his examination and earned his pilot's license in April 1859. He was 24 years old.

By all accounts, he was a skilled pilot and began a promising career. He wrote: "In due course I got my license. I was a pilot now, full-fledged. I dropped into casual employments; no misfortunes resulting, intermittent work gave place to steady and protracted engagements."

Sam articulated his love for piloting steamboats when he wrote: "Piloting on the Mississippi River was not work to me; it was play -- delightful play, vigorous play, adventurous play -- and I loved it."

Sam reveled in the freedom and control of guiding a boat along the Mississippi River. He wrote: "a pilot, in those days, was the only unfettered and entirely independent human being that lived in the earth."

Sam described the sensation colorfully in an August 25, 1866, letter to friend Will Bowen:

...all men--kings & serfs alike--are slaves to other men & to circumstance--save alone, the pilot--who comes at no man's beck and call, obeys no man's orders & scorns all men's suggestions. The king would do this thing, & would do that: but a cramped treasury overmasters him in the one case & a seditious people in the other. The Senator must hob-nob with canaille whom he despises, & banker, priest & statesman trim their actions by the breeze of the world's will & the world's opinion. It is a strange study,--a singular phenomenon, if you please, that the only real, independent & genuine gentlemen in the world go quietly up and down the Mississippi river, asking no homage of any one, seeking no popularity, no notoriety, & not caring a damn whether school keeps or not.

Piloting was the career Sam had dreamed of since he was a child. He had found his place. He wrote: "Time drifted smoothly and prosperously on, and I supposed -- and hoped -- that I was going to follow the river the rest of my days, and die at the wheel when my mission was ended."

Unfortunately, Sam's vision of his future was not to be. Only two years into his cherished career, the United States fractured into Civil War and both sides quickly focused military efforts on securing the important navigation corridor of the Mississippi River valley. Sam wrote, "But by and by the war came, commerce was suspended, my occupation was gone."

Sam Clemens' pilot's certificate.

BECOMING MARK TWAIN

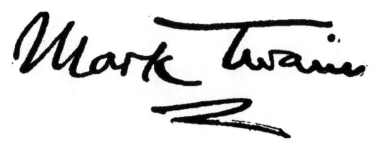

Mark Twain's signature. Courtesy of Wikimedia Commons.

As the Civil War turned the Mississippi River into a battlefield and ended commercial steamboat traffic, Sam Clemens returned to Hannibal, Missouri. He grieved the death of his brother and the loss of his beloved profession. News reports chronicled the eruption of the war between the states. So, when Sam's older brother Orion was appointed by the Lincoln administration as Secretary of the new Nevada Territory, Sam accompanied his brother to the west in 1861. Sam later summarized his adventures:

> *I had to seek another livelihood. So I became a silver miner in Nevada; next, a newspaper reporter; next, a gold miner, in California; next, a reporter in San Francisco; next, a special correspondent in the Sandwich Islands; next, a roving correspondent in Europe and the East; next, an instructional torch-*

*bearer on the lecture platform; and, finally, I became
a scribbler of books, and an immovable fixture among
the other rocks of New England.*

Even as his life journey diverted towards the west,
Sam carried with him part of his Mississippi River
experience. While working for the Nevada newspaper
Territorial Enterprise, Sam first used his now-famous
pseudonym. He had already signed some writings with
pen-names such as "Josh" and "Thomas Jefferson
Snodgrass." But in February 1863 Sam Clemens first
signed an article with the alias "Mark Twain." Perhaps
this moniker remained since it reminded him of the job
he loved best - steering a steamboat along the Mississippi
River - because "Mark Twain" is a steamboat term.

In Sam Clemens' time as a pilot, a deckhand was
assigned to assist the pilot with occasional measurements
of the depth of the water. That deck hand was known as
the "leadsman" because he used a long piece of rope with
a lead weight tied to the end. Along the rope, knots or
lashes would mark fractions of each fathom - a
measurement of six feet. Holding one end of the rope, the
leadsman would swing and hurl the lead-weighted end
of the rope out into the river ahead of the boat where it
quickly sank to the river bottom. As rope came alongside
the boat the leadsman would reel in the measurement
and shout the depth up to the pilot.

"Twain" is an old-fashioned term meaning "two" - as
in the old saying "East is East and West is West and
never the twain shall meet." The leadsman's call of

"Mark Twain" literally indicated that the pilot could mark two fathoms - a depth of 12 feet. This would have been significant to a pilot steering a boat with a draft of about six feet because it ensured that there was an additional six feet of water below the hull and that the boat was not at risk of hitting any obstruction. To steamboat pilots, the leadsman's call of "Mark Twain" indicated safe conditions to progress. Assuming the name "Mark Twain" seemed to do the same for Sam Clemens.

RIVER WRITINGS

The experiences of working on the riverboats of the Mississippi River not only shaped Twain career, but also his later writings. He gave this explanation:

> DURING the two or two and a half years of my apprenticeship, I served under many pilots, and had experience of many kinds of steamboatmen... I am to this day profiting somewhat by that experience; for in that brief, sharp schooling, I got personally and familiarly acquainted with about all the different types of human nature that are to be found in fiction, biography, or history... When I find a well-drawn character in fiction or biography, I generally take a warm personal interest in him, for the reason that I have known him before -- met him on the river.

Twain enjoyed successes in his writing career with selections such as his popular 1865 short story "The Celebrated Jumping Frog of Calaveras County" and best-selling books such as *The Innocents Abroad* and *The Gilded Age.*

In 1875, Twain recounted many of his riverboat memories in a series of seven articles for *The Atlantic* magazine entitled "Old Times on the Mississippi."

Twain drew from his childhood along the Mississippi River for his 1876 book *The Adventures of Tom Sawyer.*

Twain traveled the Mississippi River again in 1882, cruising aboard steamboats to refresh his memory. He added new material into his previous articles for *The Atlantic* magazine and published the book version as *Life on the Mississippi* in 1883.

Twain again used the river as a setting and subject for his 1885 masterpiece *Adventures of Huckleberry Finn*. That book is regarded as a great American classic. Literary legend Ernest Hemingway once even remarked, "All modern American literature comes from one book by Mark Twain called *Huckleberry Finn*."

Twain clarified his passion for piloting when *Life on the Mississippi* was published in 1883. He wrote, "If I have seemed to love my subject, it is no surprising thing, for I loved the profession far better than any I have followed since, and I took a measureless pride in it."

Twain did much of his writing while spending months of each year at his sister-in-law's estate called Quarry Farm at Elmira, New York. He worked from a custom-built cottage that mimicked a steamboat pilot house which was set on a bluff overlooking the Chemung River valley. The presence of the boats steaming along the river connected him to a passion and source of creativity. He wrote:

> *Once or twice each night, we'd see a Steamboat slipping along in the dark. And every now and again, she'd belch a whole world of sparks up out of her chimney. And they would rain down in the river and look awful pretty.*

With that familiar inspiration, Twain at Quarry Farm crafted many of his most renowned works including *Tom Sawyer, Life on the Mississippi, Huckleberry Finn, Roughing It, A Tramp Abroad, The Prince and the Pauper,* and *A Connecticut Yankee at Kings Arthur's Court.*

Twain in his writing room in Elmira, NY, courtesy of Wikimedia Commons.

LATER LIFE

Olivia Langdon in 1869, the year before she married Samuel Clemens (Mark Twain). Courtesy of Wikimedia Commons.

At the very end of 1867, Twain met Olivia Langdon, the sister of an acquaintance. He was smitten and they married on February 2, 1870. She also made a great impact on his work. He wrote:

I never wrote a serious word until after I married Mrs. Clemens. She is solely responsible - to her should go the credit - for any influence my subsequent work should exert. After my marriage, she edited everything I wrote.

Twain endured professional and personal heartbreak. Bad investments forced him to file bankruptcy late in life. But he was determined to repay his debts. To generate revenue, he embarked in the summer of 1895 on a yearlong worldwide lecture tour that included more than 100 performances in cities across the United States, Canada, Australia, New Zealand, India, and South Africa. In August 1895, after a busy start to the tour with 23 performances in 22 American and Canadian cities, Twain wrote from Vancouver, British Columbia:

Lecturing is gymnastics, chest-expander, medicine, mind healer, blues destroyer, all in one. I am twice as well as I was when I started out. I have gained nine pounds in twenty eight days, and expect to weigh six hundred before January. I haven't had a blue day in all the twenty-eight. My wife and daughter are accumulating health and strength and flesh nearly as fast as I am. When we reach home two years hence, we think we can exhibit as freaks.

His extensive travels brought him many unique experiences and taught him many lessons. He wrote:

Travel is fatal to prejudice, bigotry, and narrow-mindedness, and many of our people need it sorely on these accounts. Broad, wholesome, charitable views of men and things cannot be acquired by vegetating in one little corner of the earth all one's lifetime.

Mark Twain celebrated his seventieth birthday in 1905 at a lavish affair at Delmonico's restaurant in New York City. He gave a speech that night offering advice about achieving a long life:

I will offer here, as a sound maxim, this: That we can't reach old age by another man's road.

I have been regular about going to bed and getting up-and that is one of the main things. I have made it a rule to go to bed when there wasn't anybody left to sit up with; and I have made it a rule to get up when I had to.

In the matter of diet-which is another main thing-I have been persistently strict in sticking to the things which didn't agree with me until one or the other of us got the best of it.

I have made it a rule never to smoke more than one cigar at a time. I have no other restriction as regards smoking.

As for drinking, I have no rule about that. When the others drink I like to help;

I have never taken any exercise, except sleeping and resting, and I never intend to take any. Exercise is loathsome. And it cannot be any benefit when you are tired; and I was always tired.

We can't reach old age by another man's road. My habits protect my life, but they would assassinate you.

Despite his reputation as a humorist, Twain's personal life was filled with heartbreak. His father died when he was only 11. Four of his six siblings died early in life, including his brother Henry in a steamboat explosion. Twain adored his wife Olivia and was devastated when she died in 1904 at age 58. Twain also endured the death of three of his four children. Heartache and loss tormented him and he carried a heavy load of grief. Fatigued by the weight of those burdens, in 1909 Twain wrote this fascinating passage:

> *I came in with Halley's comet in 1835. It is coming again next year, and I expect to go out with it. It will be the greatest disappointment of my life if I don't go out with Halley's comet. The Almighty has said, no doubt: "Now here are these two unaccountable freaks; they came in together, they must go out together." Oh! I am looking forward to that.*

Halley's Comet did return the following year in 1910 and on April 20th it reached perihelion - the point of its orbit closest to the sun. The following day, on April 21, 1910, Mark Twain died.

CLOSING

Mark Twain. Courtesy of Wikimedia Commons.

For more than a century after his death, Mark Twain has remained one of the most beloved and iconic of American writers. Thomas Edison once said, "An average American loves his family. If he has any love left over for some other person, he generally selects Mark Twain." The following passage from Twain's *Life on the Mississippi* captures his passion for the river and enduring acclaim.

The face of the water, in time, became a wonderful book -- a book that was a dead language to the uneducated passenger, but which told its mind to me without reserve, delivering its most cherished secrets as clearly as if it uttered them with a voice.

Throughout the long twelve hundred miles there was never a page that was void of interest, never one that you could leave unread without loss, never one that you would want to skip, thinking you could find higher enjoyment in some other thing. There never was so wonderful a book written by man; never one whose interest was so absorbing, so unflagging, so sparklingly renewed with every reperusal.

And it was not a book to be read once and thrown aside, for it had a new story to tell every day.

My name is Bill Wiemuth and I thank you for joining me for this History Highlights book. Twain is such a fascinating person. It certainly has been my pleasure researching and sharing with you highlights of his remarkable life.

I also hope you are developing an ever-growing fascination for history. At **HistoryHighlights.com**, explore our amazing collection of books, audiobooks, and 200+ video presentations offering you fascinating true stories in less than an hour.

There is so much to explore, learn, and enjoy. I know you will savor every moment. Please tell your friends and family about History Highlights. And connect with us online to enjoy FREE eBooks, audiobooks, and video programs! Learn more at **HistoryHighlights.com.**

We have spotlighted fascinating true stories such as the international intrigue and secret deals that enabled The Louisiana Purchase. A two-book set shares the tales of the Lewis and Clark Expedition. Another book illuminates the remarkable historical role of the Mississippi River. Or explore the impact on the Civil War of the Union's Anaconda Plan, intended to cripple the South's economy by controlling the Confederate coastline and waterways. The story of the first steamboat to travel down the Mississippi River is an adventure where everything that could go wrong did go wrong. But that riveting drama changed U.S. economy and history forever.

America's history is filled with so many amazing stories to learn and explore. I know you will enjoy every moment of it. Thank you for sharing your time on this journey of discovery. Please recommend our HistoryHighlights.com books and learning programs to your friends and family. Review recent editions of our free monthly history newsletter and subscribe at **HistoryHighlights.com.**

--The End—

PLEASE – A QUICK REVIEW.

Your review of this book is one of the primary ways we expand to find a new and growing audience of readers. Please leave your review in just few seconds at this link:

https://amzn.to/46j35Sb

Thank you so much!

We have many more books available to explore and enjoy in a variety of formats including eBooks, paperbacks, audiobooks. We also have a site offering more than 200 history video presentations. Please stay in touch with us with our free weekly HistoryHighlights.com newsletter. Enjoy free books, video presentations, and special insights. Preview samples and join our journey of discovery at **HistoryHighlights.com.**

LEARN MORE

Following are just a few suggestions of resources to continue your exploration about Mark Twain. Enjoy your journey of discovery!

----BOOKS----

Life on the Mississippi
by Mark Twain

The Adventures of Tom Sawyer
by Mark Twain

Adventures of Huckleberry Finn
by Mark Twain

Autobiography of Mark Twain
by Mark Twain

Grant and Twain: The Story of a Friendship That Changed America
by Mark Perry

----VIDEOS----

"Mark Twain Tonight" featuring Hal Holbrook

"Mark Twain: A Film Directed by Ken Burns"

----ONLINE----

Biography.com online video:
https://www.biography.com/video/mark-twain-full-episode-2074654020

History Channel:
https://www.history.com/topics/art-history/mark-twain

PBS Ken Burns site
https://www.pbs.org/kenburns/mark-twain/video

UC Berkley website about Twain's river era
https://bancroft.berkeley.edu/Exhibits/MTP/mississippi.html

Smithsonian magazine article
https://www.smithsonianmag.com/travel/how-mississippi-river-made-mark-twain-and-vice-versa-180950193/

ABOUT THE AUTHOR

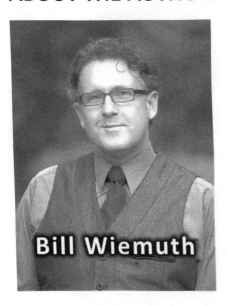

Bill Wiemuth

I have loved every moment of my study and sharing of history. In the last two decades, I have proudly written, produced, and published a diverse collection of books, audiobooks, and video presentations which highlight amazing stories from United States history.

As a speaker, I have presented these stories aboard more than 500 cruises and delivered more than 3,000 presentations for cruise lines and organizations and corporate events across the U.S. and internationally. I also have appeared for numerous regional and national radio television programs including National Public Radio, CNN's *Headline News* and ABC's *Good Morning, America*. My collection of 200+ video presentations has been published into its own online streaming video platform.

As a "reporter of the past," I value the skills I learned to earn a B.A. in Journalism from the University of Texas at Arlington. I also have earned an Alaska Naturalist certification from the University of Alaska - Southeast and I have been recognized as a Certified Interpretive Guide by the National Association of Interpretation which provides training for the National Park Service.

Learn more about me and my work to share stories from history, plus enjoy free books, audiobooks, video presentations, a weekly newsletter, and more. Visit us at **HistoryHighlights.com**.

Made in the USA
Middletown, DE
19 March 2024

51750679R00038